Courageous Female and Visionary Male:

Our Future Leaders

By Susette A. O'Neal

Copyright © 2024 Susette ONeal

All rights reserved.

ISBN:

DEDICATION

As a woman of profound faith, guided by the teachings of Jesus Christ, I understand the profound impact of Joy and Peace. To my family and friends, whose love and support make my world a happier place. To my mentors and role models, who have shown me the path to true happiness. To the seekers of joy and the believers in a better tomorrow. May you always find reasons to smile. To humanity, in hopes that we all find our path to happiness and spread joy wherever we go.

TABLE OF CONTENTS

0 Acknowledgments	6
1 Chapter Embracing Your Alpha Female Identity	7
2 Chapter Developing Leadership Skills as an Alpha Female	15
3 Chapter Navigating the Workplace as an Alpha Female	20
4 Chapter Cultivating a Supportive Network as an Alpha Female Leader	31
5 Chapter Overcoming Imposter Syndrome and Self- Doubt	37
6 Chapter Leading with Authenticity and Integrity	43
7 Chapter The Alpha Female's Guide to Work-Life Balance	49
8 Chapter Embracing Challenges and Seizing Opportunities	55
9 Chapter Empowering the Next Generation of Alpha Female Leaders	61
10 Chapter Pioneers of Innovation	68
11 Chapter Fearless Entrepreneurs	72
12 Chapter The Rise of the Titans	76
13 Chapter The Maverick Minds	80
14 Chapter The Future of Tech	84
15 Chapter Lessons from the Masters	88
16 Chapter Inspiring Stories of Triumph	93
17 Chapter The Legacy of Bold Visionaries	97
18 Chapter Conclusion	100
19 About the Author	103

Acknowledgements

I am deeply grateful to my loving family, especially my husband of 37 years and my two wonderful children, for their unwavering support and understanding throughout the process of bringing this book to life. Your encouragement and patience have been my rock. I would also like to express my gratitude to the readers who have embraced my stories with open hearts. Your enthusiasm and support mean the world to me.

1 Chapter Embracing Your Alpha Female Identity

Recognizing the Traits of an Alpha Female

In the world of leadership, the term "alpha female" is often used to describe a woman who exhibits strong, confident, and assertive traits. These women are not afraid to take charge, make tough decisions, and lead with courage and conviction. Recognizing the traits of an alpha female is essential for anyone aspiring to be a successful leader in today's competitive business world.

One key trait of an alpha female is her unwavering confidence. She believes in herself and her abilities, and this self-assurance radiates in everything she does. Whether she is leading a team meeting, negotiating a deal, or presenting a proposal, the alpha female exudes confidence and commands respect from those around her.

Another trait of an alpha female is her assertiveness. She is not afraid to speak her mind, express her opinions, and stand up for what she believes in. This assertiveness is essential for effective leadership, as it allows the alpha female to make tough decisions, set clear expectations, and hold others accountable for their actions.

In addition to confidence and assertiveness, the alpha female is also known for her resilience. She faces challenges head-on, bounces back from setbacks, and never gives up on her goals. This resilience is what sets her apart from others and allows her to overcome obstacles and achieve success in the face of adversity.

Furthermore, the alpha female is a natural born leader. She has a strong vision, inspires others to follow her lead, and is able to motivate and empower her team to achieve their full potential. Her leadership style is inclusive, collaborative, and strategic, making her a highly effective and respected leader in any organization.

Recognizing the traits of an alpha female is crucial for women who aspire to be successful leaders in today's competitive business world. By embodying confidence, assertiveness, resilience, and leadership, the alpha female can pave her path to success and inspire others to do the same. With determination, passion, and a strong sense of purpose, the alpha female can achieve her full potential and lead with confidence and courage in any leadership role she takes on.

Breaking Stereotypes: Embracing Your Strengths

In this subchapter, we will explore the concept of breaking stereotypes and embracing your strengths as an Alpha Female in leadership. As women in positions of power, we often face stereotypes and biases that can hold us back from reaching our full potential. It is essential to recognize these stereotypes and challenge them head-on by embracing our unique strengths and qualities.

One common stereotype that Alpha Females in leadership face is that they are too aggressive or assertive. Society often expects women to be passive and accommodating, but as Alpha Females, we know that being assertive and confident is not a weakness, but a strength. By embracing our assertiveness and using it to our advantage, we can effectively lead our teams and organizations towards success.

Another stereotype that Alpha Females often encounter is that they are too emotional or sensitive to lead effectively. This stereotype is rooted in the outdated belief that emotions are a sign of weakness, when in reality, emotions can be a powerful tool for leadership. By embracing our emotions and using them to connect with others on a deeper level, we can build stronger relationships and inspire our teams to achieve greatness.

It is crucial for Alpha Females in leadership to recognize and challenge these stereotypes in order to fully embrace their strengths and lead with confidence. By breaking free from these limiting beliefs, we can pave the way for future generations of women to rise to positions of power and influence. It is time to shatter the glass ceiling and show the world that Alpha Females are not bound by stereotypes but empowered by their unique strengths and qualities.

By breaking stereotypes and embracing our strengths as Alpha Females in leadership, we can lead with confidence, courage, and authenticity. It is time to redefine what it means to be a leader and show the world that women are just as capable, if not more so, than their male counterparts. Let us stand tall, speak boldly, and lead with grace, knowing that our unique strengths are what set us apart and make us unstoppable in the pursuit of our goals.

Overcoming Challenges: Dealing with Misconceptions

In the journey to becoming a successful leader, women often face many challenges and obstacles that can hinder their progress. One common challenge that alpha females in leadership roles face is dealing with misconceptions about their abilities and leadership style.

These misconceptions can come from both external sources, such as colleagues or superiors, as well as from within themselves. In order to overcome these challenges and continue to thrive as a leader, it is important for alpha females to address and challenge these misconceptions head-on.

One common misconception that alpha females in leadership roles face is that they are bossy or overly aggressive. This stereotype is often rooted in outdated gender norms and can be damaging to a woman's confidence and credibility as a leader. To overcome this misconception, it is important for alpha females to be aware of how they are perceived by others and to actively work to counteract these negative stereotypes.

This may involve adjusting their communication style, seeking feedback from colleagues, and showcasing their strengths and accomplishments in a confident and assertive manner. Another common misconception that alpha females in leadership roles face is that they are not as empathetic or nurturing as their male counterparts.

This stereotype can be particularly damaging in fields where emotional intelligence and empathy are valued, such as healthcare or education.

To overcome this misconception, alpha females can work to develop and showcase their emotional intelligence skills, communicate openly and honestly with their team members, and demonstrate empathy and understanding in their interactions with others. By actively challenging this misconception, alpha females can show that they are capable of being both strong and compassionate leaders.

In addition to external misconceptions, alpha females in leadership roles may also struggle with internal doubts and insecurities about their abilities and worthiness as a leader. This imposter syndrome can be particularly pervasive for women in male-dominated industries or environments.

To overcome these internal challenges, it is important for alpha females to cultivate self-awareness, practice self-care, and seek support from mentors and peers. By acknowledging and addressing their own doubts and insecurities, alpha females can build confidence in their leadership abilities and continue to thrive in their roles.

Overall, overcoming challenges and dealing with misconceptions is an essential part of the journey to leadership success for alpha females. By actively challenging stereotypes, developing emotional intelligence, and cultivating self-awareness, alpha females can overcome these obstacles and continue to thrive as confident and courageous leaders.

Through perseverance, self-reflection, and a commitment to growth, alpha females can rise above the challenges they face and achieve their full potential as leaders in their respective fields.

Assertiveness vs. Aggressiveness: Finding the Balance

Finding the balance between assertiveness and aggressiveness is essential for alpha females in leadership positions. By embracing assertiveness as a tool for effective communication and conflict resolution, while avoiding the pitfalls of aggressiveness, you can lead with confidence and courage.

Remember to approach conflicts with a level head, be open to feedback, and prioritize clear and respectful communication. By embodying these qualities, you can pave the way for success and inspire those around you to reach their full potential.

2 Chapter Developing Leadership Skills as an Alpha Female

Communication Strategies for Effective Leadership

Communication is a critical component of effective leadership, especially for alpha females who are striving to succeed in their leadership roles. In order to effectively lead a team, it is essential to have strong communication strategies in place. One key strategy is to be clear and concise in your communication. As an alpha female leader, it is important to convey your message in a direct and straightforward manner, so that there is no room for misinterpretation. This will help ensure that your team understands your expectations and goals and can work towards achieving them effectively.

It is also important to consider the impact of your communication style on those around you. Assertive leaders are able to express their thoughts and opinions in a clear and direct manner, while also listening actively to the perspectives of others. In contrast, aggressive leaders may come across as abrasive and dismissive, causing tension and resentment among team members. By focusing on effective communication and fostering a culture of open dialogue, you can create a harmonious and productive work environment.

Another important aspect of finding the balance between assertiveness and aggressiveness is knowing when to stand your ground and when to compromise. As an alpha female in leadership, it is essential to have a strong sense of self-confidence and conviction in your decisions. However, it is equally important to be open to feedback and willing to make adjustments when necessary. By striking a balance between being firm in your beliefs and being flexible in your approach, you can foster a positive and collaborative work environment.

Another important communication strategy for alpha female leaders is active listening. This means truly hearing and understanding what your team members are saying and taking their feedback into consideration. By actively listening to your team, you show that you value their input and are open to different perspectives. This can help build trust and rapport with your team members and create a more collaborative and supportive work environment.

In addition to being clear and concise in your communication, it is also important to be assertive when necessary. As an alpha female leader, you may encounter situations where you need to assert yourself and stand your ground. By being assertive in your communication, you can effectively communicate your boundaries and expectations, and ensure that your voice is heard. This can help prevent misunderstandings and conflicts and establish you as a strong and confident leader.

Furthermore, alpha female leaders should also be mindful of their nonverbal communication. Body language, facial expressions, and tone of voice can all convey messages to your team members, sometimes more powerfully than words. By being aware of your nonverbal communication, you can ensure that your messages are received positively and effectively. This can help you build credibility and authority as a leader and inspire confidence in your team.

Overall, effective communication is key to successful leadership for alpha females. By employing strategies such as being clear and concise, active listening, assertiveness, and mindful nonverbal communication, alpha female leaders can effectively communicate their vision, expectations, and goals to their team members. This can help build strong relationships, foster collaboration, and drive success in their leadership roles. By mastering these communication strategies, alpha female leaders can confidently and courageously lead their teams to achieve their full potential.

Building Confidence in Decision Making

In the fast-paced world of leadership, decision-making is a crucial skill that can make or break a leader. As an Alpha Female in a leadership role, it is important to build confidence in your decision-making abilities in order to lead with authority and conviction. Building confidence in decision-making starts with knowing yourself and your values. When you have a strong sense of self and are clear on what is important to you, it becomes easier to make decisions that align with your values and beliefs.

Another key aspect of building confidence in decision-making is trusting your gut instinct. As an Alpha Female, you likely have strong intuition and instincts that guide you in the right direction. Trusting these instincts can help you make quick and effective decisions, even in high-pressure situations.
Remember, your intuition is there for a reason – don't ignore it.

It is also important to seek feedback from trusted advisors and mentors when making important decisions. As an Alpha Female, you may be used to making decisions independently, but getting input from others can provide valuable insights and perspectives that you may not have considered. Surround yourself with a strong support network of people who have your best interests at heart and who can offer constructive feedback to help you make informed decisions, building confidence in decision-making requires practice and experience.

The more decisions you make, the more confident you will become in your ability to navigate complex situations and make tough choices. Don't be afraid to take risks and learn from both your successes and failures – each decision you make is an opportunity to grow and improve your decision-making skills.

Ultimately, building confidence in decision-making as an Alpha Female in leadership is about embracing your inner strength and trusting yourself to lead with courage and conviction. By knowing yourself, trusting your instincts, seeking feedback, and gaining experience, you can become a confident and courageous leader who inspires others to follow your lead.

Remember, confidence is key in decision- making – believe in yourself and your ability to make the tough calls that will propel you and your team to success.

By Susette ONeal

3 Chapter Navigating the Workplace as an Alpha Female

Handling Office Politics with Grace and Diplomacy Establishing

In the fast-paced world of corporate environments, office politics can often be a challenging aspect to navigate, especially for alpha females in leadership positions. However, it is essential to handle these situations with grace and diplomacy in order to maintain a positive work environment and ensure that your leadership is respected by your colleagues. This subchapter will provide you with valuable tips and strategies for handling office politics with confidence and poise.

First and foremost, it is important to remain calm and composed when faced with office politics. As an alpha female in leadership, you are likely to encounter situations where tensions run high, and emotions are heightened. However, by maintaining your composure and approaching these situations with a level head, you will be better able to handle conflicts and disagreements with grace and diplomacy. Remember to take a step back, assess the situation objectively, and respond in a thoughtful and strategic manner.

Communication is key when it comes to navigating office politics. As an alpha female in leadership, it is important to be clear and concise in your communication with colleagues. Be assertive yet respectful in your interactions, and always strive to find common ground and solutions that benefit the entire team. By fostering open and honest communication, you can help to prevent misunderstandings and conflicts from escalating and build stronger relationships with your colleagues in the process.

Another important aspect of handling office politics with grace and diplomacy is to stay true to your values and principles. As an alpha female in leadership, it is crucial to maintain your integrity and uphold your ethical standards, even in the face of challenging situations. By staying true to yourself and your beliefs, you will earn the respect and trust of your colleagues and demonstrate your strength and leadership capabilities.

In addition, it is important to build alliances and cultivate positive relationships with your colleagues in order to navigate office politics effectively. By establishing strong connections with key stakeholders and influencers within your organization, you can gain valuable insights and support that will help you to navigate complex office dynamics with confidence and poise. Remember to approach these relationships with authenticity and sincerity, and always strive to build trust and mutual respect with your colleagues.

Handling office politics with grace and diplomacy is a crucial skill for alpha females in leadership positions. By remaining calm and composed, communicating effectively, staying true to your values, and building alliances with your colleagues, you can navigate office politics with confidence and poise.

Remember that as a leader, your actions and attitudes will set the tone for your team, so it is important to approach office politics with professionalism and integrity at all times. By following these tips and strategies, you can navigate office politics with confidence and emerge as a strong and respected leader in your organization.

Boundaries and Setting Expectations

In order to be successful as an alpha female in leadership, it is crucial to establish boundaries and set clear expectations with those around you. Setting boundaries is not about being rigid or inflexible, but rather about communicating your needs and setting limits to protect your time, energy, and well-being. By clearly defining your boundaries, you can prevent burnout, maintain healthy relationships, and ensure that you are able to focus on your priorities.

One of the key aspects of establishing boundaries is learning to say no. As alpha females, we often feel the pressure to say yes to every request that comes our way in order to prove ourselves. However, saying yes to everything can lead to overwhelm and resentment. By setting clear boundaries around what you are willing and able to take on, you can prioritize your own needs and make space for the tasks and relationships that truly matter to you.

Setting expectations is also essential for effective leadership as an alpha female. Clearly communicating your expectations to your team, colleagues, and superiors can help prevent misunderstandings, reduce conflict, and ensure that everyone is on the same page. When people know what is expected of them, they are more likely to meet those expectations and deliver results. Additionally, setting high standards for yourself and others can help you maintain a strong sense of professionalism and excellence in your leadership role.

It is important to remember that boundaries and expectations are not set in stone and may need to be adjusted as circumstances change. As a leader, it is your responsibility to regularly review and communicate your boundaries and expectations to ensure that they are still serving you and your team effectively. By staying open to feedback and being willing to adapt, you can create a culture of transparency and trust within your team, which is essential for long-term success.

Establishing boundaries and setting clear expectations are essential practices for alpha females in leadership. By prioritizing your own needs, learning to say no, and communicating your expectations effectively, you can create a healthy and productive work environment that supports your success.

Boundaries are not about being harsh or controlling, but rather about respecting yourself and others and creating a strong foundation for leadership. By mastering the art of setting boundaries and expectations, you can confidently lead with courage and achieve your goals as an alpha female in the workplace.

Dealing with Resistance and Pushback

As an Alpha Female in a leadership position, you can expect to face resistance and pushback from those around you. Whether it's from colleagues who are threatened by your confidence and assertiveness, or from subordinates who are resistant to change, dealing with resistance is a key skill that you must develop in order to succeed in your role.

One of the most important things to remember when faced with resistance is to stay calm and composed. It can be tempting to react emotionally when someone challenges you or questions your decisions but responding with anger or defensiveness will only escalate the situation. Instead, take a deep breath and respond calmly and rationally. This will demonstrate to others that you are in control of the situation and can handle challenges with grace and poise.

Another important strategy for dealing with resistance is to listen actively to the concerns and objections of others. People are more likely to be receptive to your ideas and decisions if they feel that their opinions are being heard and respected. By listening carefully to what others have to say, you can gain valuable insights into their perspectives and address their concerns in a constructive way.

It's also important to remember that not all resistance is negative. Sometimes, pushback can actually lead to better outcomes by challenging your assumptions and forcing you to reevaluate your decisions. Instead of seeing resistance as a roadblock, try to view it as an opportunity for growth and learning. By being open-minded and receptive to feedback, you can turn resistance into a positive force for change and innovation.

Ultimately, dealing with resistance and pushback is a skill that can be developed over time with practice and patience. By staying calm, listening actively, and viewing resistance as an opportunity for growth, you can navigate the challenges of leadership with confidence and courage. Remember, as an Alpha Female, you have the strength and resilience to overcome any obstacle that comes your way.

One of the first steps in building strong relationships with mentors and allies is to identify individuals who can support and guide you on your leadership journey. Look for people who have experience and expertise in your field, as well as those who share your values and vision for success. Reach out to them, introduce yourself, and express your interest in establishing a mentorship or partnership.

Building strong relationships with mentors and allies is a crucial aspect of success for any alpha female in leadership. Mentors provide guidance, support, and valuable insights that can help you navigate the challenges of leadership with confidence and grace. Allies, on the other hand, are your partners in the journey towards achieving your goals and ambitions. They provide you with the network, resources, and connections necessary to thrive in your leadership role.

Once you have identified potential mentors and allies, it is important to cultivate these relationships with care and intention. Be proactive in seeking out their advice and feedback and be open to learning from their experiences and perspectives. Show gratitude for their time and support and be willing to reciprocate in any way that you can.

Building strong relationships with mentors and allies is a powerful tool for success as an alpha female in leadership. By seeking out guidance and support from experienced mentors, and forming partnerships with like-minded allies, you can navigate the challenges of leadership with confidence and courage. Cultivating these relationships with care, communication, and gratitude will not only benefit you personally and professionally, but also contribute to your growth and success as a leader.

Communication is key to building strong relationships with mentors and allies. Be transparent about your goals, challenges, and aspirations, and keep them updated on your progress and achievements. Seek their input and feedback on important decisions and be open to constructive criticism and guidance. Building trust and rapport with your mentors and allies is essential for a successful and fulfilling relationship.

Finding Your Tribe: Connecting with Like-Minded Women

In the journey to leadership success, one of the most important factors is finding your tribe - a group of like-minded women who can support and uplift you on your path. As an alpha female in leadership, it can be challenging to find women who understand your unique strengths and struggles. However, connecting with other alpha females can be incredibly empowering and beneficial to your growth as a leader.

When looking for your tribe, it's important to seek out women who share your values, goals, and ambitions. Surrounding yourself with like-minded women who are driven, ambitious, and fearless can help you stay motivated and inspired. These women will understand your drive for success and can provide valuable insights and advice based on their own experiences.

However, alpha females must be careful not to let their compassion overshadow their leadership abilities. It is important to set boundaries and make tough decisions, when necessary, even if it means facing conflict or confrontation. Balancing empathy with assertiveness is key to maintaining respect and authority within a leadership role.

One way for alpha females to balance leadership with empathy and compassion is to lead by example. By demonstrating kindness, understanding, and emotional intelligence in their own behavior, they can inspire their team members to do the same. This creates a culture of empathy and compassion within the organization, which can lead to a more positive and productive work environment.

Finding your tribe is not just about networking - it's about building meaningful relationships with women who truly understand and support you. Whether you connect with other alpha females through professional organizations, networking events, or social media groups, it's important to nurture these relationships and create a sense of community. By building strong connections with like-minded women, you can create a support system that will help you navigate the challenges of leadership with confidence and courage.

Finding your tribe of like-minded women is essential for the success of an alpha female in leadership. By connecting with women who share your values, goals, and ambitions, you can create a support system that will empower you to lead with confidence and courage. Through collaboration, mentorship, and mutual support, your tribe can help you navigate the challenges of leadership and achieve your full potential as a leader. So, don't be afraid to reach out and connect with other alpha females - together, you can conquer the world.

Balancing Leadership with Empathy and Compassion

Being part of a tribe of like-minded women can also provide you with opportunities for collaboration and growth. By surrounding yourself with women who are equally ambitious and driven, you can push each other to reach new heights of success.

Whether it's collaborating on projects, sharing resources, or offering mentorship and support, your tribe can help you achieve your goals and overcome obstacles in your path to leadership success.

In the world of leadership, the idea of balancing strength and compassion can often be seen as a delicate dance. For alpha females in leadership positions, this balance can be especially challenging.
On one hand, they are expected to exude confidence, assertiveness, and decisiveness. On the other hand, they are also called upon to show empathy, understanding, and

compassion towards their team members. Finding the right balance between these two qualities is crucial for effective leadership. Being a strong leader does not mean being unfeeling or unemotional.

In fact, showing empathy and compassion towards others can actually strengthen a leader's position. When team members feel that their leader truly cares about their well-being, they are more likely to be motivated, engaged, and committed to their work. This can lead to higher levels of productivity, collaboration, and overall success for the team.

Finding the right balance between leadership and empathy is crucial for alpha females in leadership positions. By combining strength with compassion, alpha females can create a powerful and effective leadership style that inspires their team members to reach their full potential. Striking this balance may require practice, self-awareness, and reflection, but the rewards can be immense in terms of team morale, productivity, and overall success.

4 Chapter Cultivating a Supportive Network as an Alpha Female Leader

Building Strong Relationships with Mentors and Allies

One of the first steps in building strong relationships with mentors and allies is to identify individuals who can support and guide you on your leadership journey. Look for people who have experience and expertise in your field, as well as those who share your values and vision for success. Reach out to them, introduce yourself, and express your interest in establishing a mentorship or partnership.

Building strong relationships with mentors and allies is a crucial aspect of success for any alpha female in leadership. Mentors provide guidance, support, and valuable insights that can help you navigate the challenges of leadership with confidence and grace. Allies, on the other hand, are your partners in the journey towards achieving your goals and ambitions. They provide you with the network, resources, and connections necessary to thrive in your leadership role.

Once you have identified potential mentors and allies, it is important to cultivate these relationships with care and intention. Be proactive in seeking out their advice and feedback and be open to learning from their experiences and perspectives. Show gratitude for their time and support and be willing to reciprocate in any way that you can.

Building strong relationships with mentors and allies is a powerful tool for success as an alpha female in leadership.

By seeking out guidance and support from experienced mentors, and forming partnerships with like-minded allies, you can navigate the challenges of leadership with confidence and courage. Cultivating these relationships with care, communication, and gratitude will not only benefit you personally and professionally, but also contribute to your growth and success as a leader.

Communication is key to building strong relationships with mentors and allies. Be transparent about your goals, challenges, and aspirations, and keep them updated on your progress and achievements. Seek their input and feedback on important decisions and be open to constructive criticism and guidance. Building trust and rapport with your mentors and allies is essential for a successful and fulfilling relationship.

Finding Your Tribe: Connecting with Like-Minded Women

In the journey to leadership success, one of the most important factors is finding your tribe - a group of like-minded women who can support and uplift you on your path. As an alpha female in leadership, it can be challenging to find women who understand your unique strengths and struggles. However, connecting with other alpha females can be incredibly empowering and beneficial to your growth as a leader.

When looking for your tribe, it's important to seek out women who share your values, goals, and ambitions. Surrounding yourself with like-minded women who are driven, ambitious, and fearless can help you stay motivated and inspired. These women will understand your drive for success and can provide valuable insights and advice based on their own experiences.

However, alpha females must be careful not to let their compassion overshadow their leadership abilities. It is important to set boundaries and make tough decisions when necessary, even if it means facing conflict or confrontation. Balancing empathy with assertiveness is key to maintaining respect and authority within a leadership role.

One way for alpha females to balance leadership with empathy and compassion is to lead by example. By demonstrating kindness, understanding, and emotional intelligence in their own behavior, they can inspire their team members to do the same. This creates a culture of empathy and compassion within the organization, which can lead to a more positive and productive work environment.

Finding your tribe is not just about networking - it's about building meaningful relationships with women who truly understand and support you. Whether you connect with other alpha females through professional organizations, networking events, or social media groups, it's important to nurture these relationships and create a sense of community. By building strong connections with like-minded women, you can create a support system that will help you navigate the challenges of leadership with confidence and courage.

Finding your tribe of like-minded women is essential for

the success of an alpha female in leadership. By connecting with women who share your values, goals, and ambitions, you can create a support system that will empower you to lead with confidence and courage. Through collaboration, mentorship, and mutual support, your tribe can help you navigate the challenges of leadership and achieve your full potential as a leader. So, don't be afraid to reach out and connect with other alpha females - together, you can conquer the world.

Balancing Leadership with Empathy and Compassion

Being part of a tribe of like-minded women can also provide you with opportunities for collaboration and growth. By surrounding yourself with women who are equally ambitious and driven, you can push each other to reach new heights of success.

Whether it's collaborating on projects, sharing resources, or offering mentorship and support, your tribe can help you achieve your goals and overcome obstacles in your path to leadership success.

In the world of leadership, the idea of balancing strength and compassion can often be seen as a delicate dance. For alpha females in leadership positions, this balance can be especially challenging.

On one hand, they are expected to exude confidence, assertiveness, and decisiveness. On the other hand, they are also called upon to show empathy, understanding, and compassion towards their team members. Finding the right balance between these two qualities is crucial for effective leadership.

Being a strong leader does not mean being unfeeling or unemotional. In fact, showing empathy and compassion towards others can actually strengthen a leader's position. When team members feel that their leader truly cares about their well-being, they are more likely to be motivated, engaged, and committed to their work. This can lead to higher levels of productivity, collaboration, and overall success for the team.

Finding the right balance between leadership and empathy is crucial for alpha females in leadership positions. By combining strength with compassion, alpha females can create a powerful and effective leadership style that inspires their team members to reach their full potential. Striking this balance may require practice, self-awareness, and reflection, but the rewards can be immense in terms of team morale, productivity, and overall success.

5 Chapter Overcoming Imposter Syndrome and Self-Doubt

Recognizing and Addressing Imposter Syndrome

Imposter syndrome is a common phenomenon that many women, especially those in leadership roles, experience. It is characterized by feelings of self-doubt and inadequacy, despite evidence of success and competence. Recognizing and addressing imposter syndrome is crucial for alpha females in leadership positions to reach their full potential and lead with confidence.

One way to recognize imposter syndrome is to pay attention to your inner dialogue. Do you often doubt your abilities or second-guess your decisions? Do you feel like you don't deserve your success or that you are just lucky? These are all signs of imposter syndrome. By becoming aware of these negative thought patterns, you can start to challenge them and replace them with more positive and empowering beliefs.

Addressing imposter syndrome requires taking action to build confidence and self-esteem. One strategy is to keep a success journal, where you write down your achievements and positive feedback from others. This can serve as a reminder of your skills and accomplishments, helping to counteract feelings of self- doubt. Additionally, seeking out mentorship and support from other successful women can help you gain perspective and encouragement in moments of doubt.

Another effective way to combat imposter syndrome is to practice self-compassion. Instead of being overly critical of yourself, try to treat yourself with kindness and understanding. Remind yourself that no one is perfect and that it is okay to make mistakes. By cultivating a more compassionate attitude towards yourself, you can build resilience and bounce back from setbacks with greater strength and grace.

Recognizing and addressing imposter syndrome is essential for alpha females in leadership positions to thrive and lead with confidence. By paying attention to your inner dialogue, taking action to build confidence, seeking support from others, and practicing self-compassion, you can overcome feelings of self-doubt and imposter syndrome. Remember, you are capable, deserving, and worthy of success. Embrace your strengths, own your accomplishments, and lead with courage and confidence as the alpha female you are meant to be.

Embracing Vulnerability as a Strength

In the world of leadership, there is often a misconception that showing vulnerability is a sign of weakness. However, embracing vulnerability can actually be a powerful strength for alpha females in leadership roles. By allowing ourselves to be vulnerable, we open ourselves up to deeper connections with our team members and foster an environment of trust and authenticity.

One of the key benefits of embracing vulnerability as an alpha female leader is that it allows us to be more relatable and approachable to those we lead. When we are open about our own struggles and challenges, we show our team members that it is okay to be imperfect and that it is okay to ask for help. This creates a culture of support and collaboration within the team, leading to increased morale and productivity.

Furthermore, embracing vulnerability can also help us to better understand and connect with our team members on a personal level. When we show vulnerability, we are able to empathize with others and create a safe space for them to share their own struggles and concerns. This can help us to build stronger relationships with our team members and create a more inclusive and supportive work environment.

Additionally, embracing vulnerability can lead to better decision-making as a leader. When we are willing to admit our mistakes and seek feedback from others, we are able to learn and grow from our experiences. This vulnerability allows us to make more informed decisions and avoid repeating past errors, ultimately leading to greater success for ourselves and our team.

Embracing vulnerability as an alpha female in leadership is not a sign of weakness, but rather a sign of strength and courage. By allowing ourselves to be vulnerable, we can create a more authentic and supportive work environment, build stronger relationships with our team members, and make better decisions as leaders. So let us embrace vulnerability as a strength and watch as our leadership success grows.

Practicing Self-Care and Self-Compassion

In the fast-paced world of leadership, it's easy for women, especially alpha females, to put their own well- being on the back burner. However, it's essential for these powerful women to prioritize self-care and self-compassion in order to maintain their confidence, courage, and effectiveness in their roles.

Practicing self-care involves taking the time to nurture your physical, mental, and emotional health. It means setting boundaries, saying no when necessary, and making time for activities that bring you joy and relaxation.

Self-compassion is another crucial aspect of self-care for alpha female leaders. It involves treating yourself with kindness, understanding, and forgiveness, especially in moments of failure or setback. Instead of being overly critical or judgmental of yourself, practicing self-compassion involves showing yourself the same empathy and support that you would offer to a friend. This can help you build resilience, bounce back from challenges, and maintain a positive mindset even in the face of adversity.

One way to practice self-care and self-compassion as an alpha female leader is to prioritize your physical health. This includes getting regular exercise, eating nutritious foods, and getting enough sleep. Taking care of your body not only improves your physical well-being but also boosts your mental and emotional health, giving you the energy and stamina, you need to lead with confidence and clarity.

Another important aspect of self-care and self-compassion for alpha female leaders is setting boundaries and learning to say no when necessary. As natural caretakers and high achievers, alpha females often have a tendency to take on too much and neglect their own needs. Learning to prioritize your own well- being and set limits on your time and energy is essential for maintaining balance and avoiding burnout in your leadership role.

Practicing self-care and self-compassion is not a luxury for alpha female leaders—it's a necessity. By taking care of yourself physically, mentally, and emotionally, setting boundaries, and treating yourself with kindness and understanding, you can maintain your confidence, courage, and effectiveness as a leader. Remember, you can't pour from an empty cup, so make self-care a priority in your leadership journey.

6 Chapter Leading with Authenticity and Integrity

In addition to the internal benefits, embracing diversity

and inclusion in leadership also helps to improve external relationships with customers and stakeholders. By demonstrating a commitment to diversity, we can build trust and credibility with a diverse range of audiences, including customers, investors, and the community at large. This can help to enhance our brand reputation and position us as a progressive and socially responsible organization. By showing that we value diversity and inclusion, we can attract top talent, drive innovation, and gain a competitive edge in the marketplace.

As Alpha Females in leadership, it is important for us to lead by example and champion diversity and inclusion within our organizations. This means actively seeking out diverse perspectives, promoting inclusive practices, and advocating for equality and fairness in all aspects of our work. By taking a proactive approach to diversity and inclusion, we can create a culture that celebrates differences and fosters a sense of belonging for all employees. This can help to break down barriers, challenge stereotypes, and create a more inclusive and equitable workplace for everyone.

Embracing diversity and inclusion in leadership is not just a moral imperative, but a strategic advantage for Alpha Females looking to succeed in today's global marketplace. By fostering a culture of inclusion, we can tap into the full potential of our diverse workforce, drive innovation, and build stronger relationships with customers and stakeholders. As leaders, it is up to us to set the tone and create a workplace where everyone feels valued, respected, and empowered to contribute their unique perspectives. By embracing diversity and inclusion, we can unleash the full power of our teams and create a more successful and sustainable future for our organizations.

Inspiring Others through Your Authentic Leadership Style

Staying True to Your Values and Beliefs

As an Alpha Female in leadership, it is crucial to stay true to your values and beliefs in order to maintain your authenticity and integrity. In a world where expectations and pressures can lead us to compromise our principles, it is important to remember who you are and what you stand for. Your values and beliefs are the foundation of your leadership style, and they guide your decisions and actions.

One way to stay true to your values and beliefs is to regularly assess and reflect on them. Take the time to think about what is truly important to you and what principles you want to uphold in your leadership role. By staying connected to your values, you can ensure that your actions are aligned with your beliefs, and you can lead with confidence and conviction.

It is also important to communicate your values and beliefs to those around you. By being transparent about what you stand for, you can build trust and credibility with your team and colleagues. When others see that you are consistent in your values and beliefs, they will be more likely to respect and follow your leadership.

In times of challenge or adversity, it can be tempting to compromise your values in order to achieve a desired outcome. However, staying true to your beliefs even in di cult situations is a true test of your leadership. By remaining steadfast in your principles, you can inspire others to do the same and lead by example.

Ultimately, staying true to your values and beliefs is essential for your success as an Alpha Female in leadership. By maintaining your authenticity and integrity, you can build trust, inspire others, and lead with confidence and courage. Remember, your values are what define you as a leader, so hold them close and let them guide you on your path to success.

Embracing Diversity and Inclusion in Leadership

Embracing Diversity and Inclusion in Leadership is a crucial aspect of being a successful Alpha Female in today's fast-paced and ever-changing world. As leaders, it is important to recognize the value that diversity brings to the table and to create an inclusive environment where all voices are heard and respected. By embracing diversity, we can tap into a wide range of perspectives and experiences that can help us make more informed decisions and drive innovation within our organizations.

One of the key benefits of embracing diversity and inclusion in leadership is that it helps to create a more engaged and motivated workforce. When employees feel valued and included, they are more likely to feel a sense of belonging and loyalty to the organization. This can lead to higher levels of employee satisfaction, productivity, and retention, ultimately contributing to the overall success of the company. By fostering a culture of inclusion, we can create a more dynamic and collaborative work environment that empowers individuals to reach their full potential.

As an alpha female in leadership, it is important to recognize the power of authenticity in inspiring others to follow your lead. Your unique leadership style, grounded in your values, beliefs, and experiences, can serve as a powerful source of inspiration for those around you. By embracing your authentic self and leading from a place of honesty and integrity, you can create a culture of trust and respect within your team.

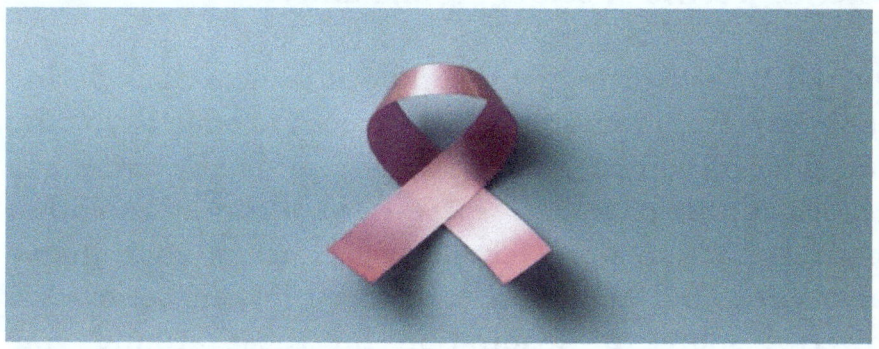

One of the key ways to inspire others through your authentic leadership style is by leading by example. Show your team members what it means to be true to yourself, even in the face of challenges and adversity. By demonstrating your own vulnerability and humanity, you can encourage others to do the same and create a more open and supportive work environment.

Another important aspect of inspiring others through your authentic leadership style is by being transparent and honest in your communication. Share your vision, goals, and values with your team members, and be open to feedback and input from others. By creating a culture of transparency and open communication, you can build trust and collaboration within your team, inspiring others to follow your lead.

In addition, it is important to lead with empathy and compassion in your interactions with others. By showing understanding and support for your team members' strengths, weaknesses, and challenges, you can inspire them to do their best work and reach their full potential. By leading with empathy and compassion, you can create a culture of inclusivity and support within your team, fostering a sense of belonging and unity.

Overall, by embracing your authentic leadership style and leading with honesty, transparency, empathy, and compassion, you can inspire others to do the same and create a culture of trust, respect, and collaboration within your team. As an alpha female in leadership, your unique perspective and approach to leadership can serve as a powerful source of inspiration for those around you, empowering them to embrace their own authentic selves and reach their full potential.

7 Chapter The Alpha Female's Guide to Work-Life Balance

Prioritizing Self-Care and Well-Being

In the fast-paced world of leadership, it can be easy for women to neglect their own well-being in favor of focusing on their career and the needs of others. However, prioritizing self-care is essential for maintaining both physical and mental health, as well as ensuring long-term success in leadership roles. By taking the time to care for ourselves, we can increase our resilience, reduce stress, and improve our overall performance as leaders.

One key aspect of self-care for alpha females in leadership is setting boundaries. It is important to recognize when we are taking on too much and learn to say no when necessary. By setting boundaries, we can prevent burnout and ensure that we have the energy and mental clarity to effectively lead our teams. This may involve delegating tasks, asking for help when needed, or simply taking time off to recharge.

Another important aspect of self-care is maintaining a healthy work-life balance. As leaders, we often feel pressure to be constantly available and working long hours. However, it is important to remember that taking time for ourselves and our families is crucial for overall well-being. By setting aside time for hobbies, exercise, and relaxation, we can recharge our batteries and come back to work refreshed and ready to tackle challenges.

Physical health is also a key component of self-care for alpha females in leadership. Regular exercise, a healthy diet, and sufficient sleep are essential for maintaining both physical and mental health. By prioritizing our physical well-being, we can increase our energy levels, improve our focus, and reduce our risk of burnout.

Making time for exercise and healthy eating may require some planning and prioritization, but the benefits far outweigh the effort.

Prioritizing self-care and well-being is essential for alpha females in leadership to thrive in their roles. By setting boundaries, maintaining a healthy work-life balance, and prioritizing physical health, we can increase our resilience, reduce stress, and improve our overall performance as leaders.

Remember, taking care of yourself is not selfish – it is necessary for long-term success and fulfilment in both your personal and professional life.

Setting Boundaries to Maintain Balance

Setting boundaries is crucial for maintaining balance in all aspects of life. As an alpha female in a leadership role, it can be easy to get caught up in the demands of the job and neglect your personal well- being. By setting boundaries, you can ensure that you are taking care of yourself while also excelling in your leadership role.

One way to set boundaries is to establish clear expectations with your team. Let them know what you need from them in terms of communication, deadlines, and workload. By setting these expectations early on, you can prevent misunderstandings and ensure that everyone is on the same page.

It's also important to set boundaries with yourself. This means knowing when to say no to additional responsibilities or commitments that may take away from your focus and energy. It's okay to prioritize your own well-being and not overextend yourself.

Setting boundaries can also help you maintain a healthy work-life balance. As an alpha female in a leadership role, it can be easy to let work consume your life. By setting boundaries around when you work and when you take time for yourself, you can prevent burnout and ensure that you are able to show up as your best self in both your personal and professional life.

Setting boundaries is essential for maintaining balance as an alpha female in a leadership role. By establishing clear expectations with your team, setting boundaries with yourself, and prioritizing your well-being, you can ensure that you are able to excel in your leadership role while also taking care of yourself. Remember, it's not selfish to set boundaries – it's necessary for your success and well-being.

Finding Fulfillment and Joy in Both Career and Personal Life

As Alpha Females in leadership roles, it can sometimes feel like we are constantly juggling the demands of our career and personal life. It can be overwhelming to try to find fulfilment and joy in both areas, but it is possible with the right mindset and strategies in place. In this subchapter, we will explore how to navigate the challenges of balancing career and personal life while still finding fulfilment and joy in both.

One key aspect of finding fulfilment and joy in both career and personal life is setting boundaries. As Alpha Females, we tend to be driven and ambitious, always striving to do more and be better. However, it is important to recognize when we are spreading ourselves too thin and need to set boundaries to protect our time and energy. By setting boundaries in both our career and personal life, we can create space for activities and relationships that bring us joy and fulfilment.

Another important aspect of finding fulfilment and joy in both career and personal life is prioritizing self-care. It is easy to neglect our own well-being when we are focused on achieving our career goals or taking care of others.

However, self-care is essential for maintaining our physical, emotional, and mental health. By prioritizing self-care activities such as exercise, meditation, and hobbies, we can recharge and rejuvenate ourselves, allowing us to show up as our best selves in both our career and personal life.

Additionally, finding fulfilment and joy in both career and personal life requires us to cultivate gratitude and mindfulness. It is easy to get caught up in the hustle and bustle of our daily lives, always looking towards the next goal or achievement.

However, taking the time to practice gratitude and mindfulness can help us appreciate the present moment and find joy in the little things.

By cultivating a sense of gratitude for our

accomplishments and relationships, we can find fulfilment and joy in both our career and personal life. Finding fulfilment and joy in both career and personal life as Alpha Females in leadership roles is possible with the right mindset and strategies.

By setting boundaries, prioritizing self-care, and cultivating gratitude and mindfulness, we can create a balanced and fulfilling life that brings us joy and satisfaction. Remember, it is important to prioritize your well-being and happiness in order to show up as a confident and courageous leader in both your career and personal life.

8 Chapter Embracing Challenges and Seizing Opportunities

Turning Setbacks into Opportunities for Growth

One of the main reasons why taking risks is important for the Alpha Female in Leadership is because it allows us to push past our fears and limitations. By stepping outside of our comfort zones, we are able to challenge ourselves and discover what we are truly capable of. Taking risks also opens up new opportunities for growth and success that we may not have otherwise considered. It is important to remember that failure is not the end, but rather a stepping stone towards greater achievements.

Embracing change is another essential quality for the Alpha Female in Leadership. In today's fast-paced business world, it is crucial to be adaptable and open to new ideas and ways of doing things. Those who resist change will quickly fall behind, while those who embrace it will stay ahead of the curve. Embracing change also allows us to stay relevant and competitive in our industries, as we are constantly evolving and improving ourselves and our businesses.

One way to turn setbacks into opportunities for growth is to reflect on the situation and identify what went wrong. By taking the time to analyze the setback, we can gain valuable insights into our own strengths and weaknesses as leaders. This self-reflection can help us identify areas for improvement and develop strategies to overcome similar challenges in the future. By approaching setbacks with a proactive mindset, we can transform them into valuable learning opportunities that ultimately make us better leaders.

As Alpha Females in leadership roles, setbacks are inevitable. However, it is crucial to remember that setbacks can actually serve as opportunities for growth and development. Instead of letting setbacks discourage us, we should view them as challenges that can help us become stronger and more resilient leaders. By adopting a growth mindset, we can turn setbacks into valuable learning experiences that propel us forward in our leadership journey.

As Alpha Females in Leadership, we must also be willing to take risks and embrace change in order to inspire and motivate those around us. By demonstrating our willingness to step outside of our comfort zones and try new things, we show our teams that it is okay to take risks and make mistakes. This creates a culture of innovation and creativity within our organizations, leading to greater success and growth for everyone involved.

Taking risks and embracing change are essential qualities for the Alpha Female in Leadership. By stepping outside of our comfort zones and being open to new ideas and ways of doing things, we are able to push past our fears and limitations, grow and achieve our goals, and inspire and motivate those around us. It is only by taking risks and embracing change that we can truly reach our full potential as leaders.

Seizing Leadership Opportunities and Making an Impact

Another effective way to turn setbacks into opportunities for growth is to seek feedback from others. By soliciting input from colleagues, mentors, or trusted advisors, we can gain valuable perspectives on the situation and identify areas for improvement. Constructive feedback can help us see the setback from different angles and gain new insights that we may not have considered on our own. By leveraging the wisdom of others, we can turn setbacks into opportunities for personal and professional growth.

It is also important to remember that setbacks are not a reflection of our worth as leaders. Instead of letting setbacks define us, we should view them as temporary obstacles that we have the power to overcome. By maintaining a positive attitude and focusing on solutions rather than problems, we can navigate setbacks with confidence and grace. As Alpha Females in leadership roles, we have the resilience and determination to turn setbacks into opportunities for growth and emerge even stronger on the other side.

Setbacks are a natural part of the leadership journey, but they do not have to hold us back. By adopting a growth mindset, seeking feedback from others, and maintaining a positive attitude, we can turn setbacks into opportunities for growth and development. As Alpha Females in leadership roles, we have the strength and resilience to overcome challenges and emerge as even more confident and courageous leaders. By viewing setbacks as opportunities for growth, we can continue to thrive and succeed in our leadership roles.

Taking Risks and Embracing Change

Taking Risks and Embracing Change are two key components of success for the Alpha Female in

Leadership. As women in leadership positions, it is important to step out of our comfort zones and take calculated risks in order to grow and achieve our goals. Embracing change is also crucial, as the business world is constantly evolving and those who are able to adapt and innovate will thrive in this environment.

In the competitive world of leadership, it is crucial for alpha females to seize every opportunity that comes their way in order to make a lasting impact. By taking charge and stepping into leadership roles, women can show their strength, intelligence, and unique qualities that set them apart from their male counterparts. It is essential for alpha females to be confident and courageous in order to lead effectively and inspire those around them.

One of the key ways for alpha females to seize leadership opportunities is to be proactive and assertive in their approach. Instead of waiting for opportunities to come to them, they should actively seek out chances to showcase their leadership skills and make a difference in their organizations. By taking the initiative and stepping up to the plate, alpha females can prove their worth and demonstrate their capabilities as strong and capable leaders.

Another important aspect of seizing leadership opportunities is being willing to take risks and step outside of one's comfort zone. Alpha females should not be afraid to challenge themselves and push the boundaries of what is possible. By being open to new experiences and embracing change, women can grow and develop as leaders, making a lasting impact on their teams and organizations.

Furthermore, alpha females should not be afraid to speak up and make their voices heard in leadership positions. It is important for women to share their ideas, opinions, and perspectives in order to drive positive change and innovation within their organizations. By being confident in their abilities and unafraid to express themselves, alpha females can inspire and motivate those around them to do the same.

Ultimately, by seizing leadership opportunities and making an impact, alpha females can pave the way for future generations of women in leadership roles. By setting a strong example and demonstrating their capabilities as confident and courageous leaders, women can break down barriers and shatter glass ceilings, creating a more inclusive and diverse workplace for all.

With determination, resilience, and a commitment to excellence, alpha females can achieve great success and make a lasting impact in the world of leadership.

9 Chapter Empowering the Next Generation of Alpha Female Leaders

Mentoring and Supporting Young Women in

Leadership

Mentoring and supporting young women in leadership is crucial in empowering the next generation of female leaders. As alpha females, it is our responsibility to lift up and guide younger women as they navigate their own paths to success. By sharing our knowledge, experiences, and insights, we can help them develop the confidence and courage needed to excel in leadership roles.

One way to mentor and support young women in leadership is by providing them with opportunities for growth and development. This could include offering them challenging assignments, introducing them to key contacts in your network, or recommending them for leadership development programs. By actively investing in their professional growth, you can help them build the skills and confidence they need to succeed in leadership roles.

Another important aspect of mentoring and supporting young women in leadership is providing them with emotional support and encouragement. As alpha females, we understand the challenges and obstacles that women face in the workplace. By offering a listening ear, providing guidance, and offering words of encouragement, we can help young women navigate these challenges and stay focused on their goals.

Additionally, mentoring and supporting young women in leadership involves setting a positive example for them to follow. By demonstrating strong leadership skills, resilience, and a commitment to personal and professional growth, we can inspire and motivate them to strive for excellence in their own careers. Leading by example is a powerful way to show young women what is possible when they embrace their own potential and step into leadership roles with confidence and courage.

Mentoring and supporting young women in leadership is essential for building a strong pipeline of female leaders. As alpha females, it is our duty to empower and uplift the next generation of women in leadership.

Advocating for Gender Equality and Inclusion

By providing opportunities for growth, offering emotional support, and setting a positive example, we can help young women develop the skills and confidence needed to succeed in leadership roles.
Together, we can create a more inclusive and diverse workplace where all women have the opportunity to thrive and lead with confidence and courage.

In today's fast-paced world, advocating for gender equality and inclusion is more important than ever. As alpha females in leadership positions, it is our responsibility to pave the way for future generations of women and ensure that they have the same opportunities as their male counterparts. By advocating for gender equality, we can create a more inclusive and diverse workplace that fosters creativity, innovation, and collaboration.

One of the key ways to advocate for gender equality and

inclusion is to lead by example. As alpha females, we are often seen as role models for other women in the workplace. By demonstrating confidence, courage, and resilience, we can inspire other women to step into leadership roles and break through the glass ceiling. We can also mentor and support other women in their career journeys, helping them navigate the challenges and obstacles that may come their way.

Another important way to advocate for gender equality and inclusion is to speak up and challenge the status quo. As alpha females, we have a unique platform and voice that can be used to address issues of gender inequality and discrimination in the workplace. By speaking out against sexism, bias, and inequality, we can create a more inclusive and equitable work environment for all employees. We can also advocate for policies and initiatives that promote gender equality, such as equal pay, parental leave, and flexible work arrangements.

In addition to leading by example and speaking up, alpha females can also use their influence and power to effect change on a larger scale. By partnering with other like-minded individuals and organizations, we can advocate for gender equality and inclusion in our industries and communities. We can participate in conferences, panels, and events that promote diversity and inclusion, and we can use our networks to amplify the voices of other women and marginalized groups. By leveraging our resources and connections, we can create lasting change that benefits all members of our society.

Ultimately, advocating for gender equality and inclusion

is not just a moral imperative – it is also a strategic business decision. Research has shown that companies with diverse leadership teams and inclusive work environments are more innovative, productive, and profitable.

By championing gender equality in our organizations, we can drive positive change, attract top talent, and create a culture of respect and empowerment. As alpha females in leadership positions, we have the power to shape the future of work and society – let's use that power to advocate for a more equal and inclusive world for all.

As Alpha Females in leadership positions, it is important for us to consider the legacy we leave behind. By focusing on empowerment and inspiration, we can ensure that our impact is lasting and meaningful. Leaving a legacy of empowerment means lifting up those around us, helping them to realize their own potential and strengths. By empowering others, we create a ripple effect of positivity and success that can last for generations to come.

One way to leave a legacy of empowerment is to mentor and support other women in their leadership journeys. By sharing our own experiences and offering guidance, we can help others to navigate the challenges and obstacles they may face.

By investing in the success of those around us, we create a culture of support and collaboration that benefits everyone. Empowering others also means giving them the tools and resources they need to succeed, whether that be through training, networking opportunities, or simply a listening ear.

Inspiration is another key component of leaving a lasting legacy. By living authentically and fearlessly, we can inspire others to do the same. When we show courage and confidence in our decisions and actions, we demonstrate that anything is possible. By sharing our stories of success and overcoming adversity, we can inspire others to persevere in the face of their own challenges. By being a beacon of inspiration, we can motivate others to reach for their dreams and achieve their full potential.

As Alpha Females, we have a unique opportunity to leave a legacy that empowers and inspires those who come after us. By embodying the qualities of confidence, courage, and leadership, we can set an example for others to follow.

By investing in the success of those around us and sharing our stories of triumph, we can create a legacy that will endure long after we are gone. Let us strive to leave a legacy of empowerment and inspiration, so that future generations of women leaders can continue to thrive and succeed.

Leaving a legacy of empowerment and inspiration is a powerful way to impact the world around us. As Alpha

Females in leadership positions, we have a responsibility to lift up those around us and inspire others to reach for their dreams.

By mentoring and supporting other women, we can create a culture of empowerment that benefits everyone. By living authentically and fearlessly, we can inspire others to do the same. Let us strive to leave a legacy that empowers and inspires, so that our impact will be felt long after we are gone.

Setting goals for continued growth and success is key to maintaining momentum and pushing yourself to new heights. Whether it is mastering a new skill, taking on a new challenge, or pursuing a promotion, it is important to set goals that will stretch you out of your comfort zone and propel you forward.

Remember, the journey to success is not always easy, but with determination and perseverance, you can achieve anything you set your mind to.

Lastly, I encourage you to inspire others to embrace their alpha female identity and lead with confidence. As a leader, you have the power to influence and empower those around you, so use that influence to lift others up and help them realize their full potential. By sharing your own experiences and offering guidance and support, you can create a community of strong, confident women who are unafraid to take on any challenge that comes their way.

By Susette ONeal

10 Chapter Pioneers of Innovation

The Visionaries of Silicon Valley

In the world of technology, Silicon Valley is often seen as

the epicenter of innovation and progress. It is here that some of the most influential and visionary men have made their mark on the industry, shaping the future of tech in bold and daring ways. These men are not afraid to take risks and push the boundaries of what is possible, making them true pioneers in their field.

One such visionary is Elon Musk, the CEO of Tesla and SpaceX. Musk is known for his ambitious goals and his willingness to take on projects that others may see as impossible. From his vision of colonizing Mars to his groundbreaking work in electric vehicles, Musk has shown time and time again that he is not afraid to think big and dream even bigger.

His confidence and courage have inspired countless

others in the tech industry to follow in his footsteps.

Another bold visionary in Silicon Valley is Jeff Bezos, the founder, and CEO of Amazon. Bezos has revolutionized the way we shop and consume goods, creating a company that has become a household name around the world. His relentless drive and determination have propelled Amazon to new heights, making it one of the most valuable companies in the world. Bezos's boldness in taking risks and his unwavering confidence in his vision have set him apart as a true leader in the tech industry.

These visionaries of Silicon Valley are not afraid to challenge the status quo and disrupt traditional industries. They are constantly pushing the boundaries of what is possible, seeking out new opportunities and taking risks that others may shy away from. Their confidence and courage have propelled them to the top of their field, inspiring others to follow in their footsteps and take on the challenges of the tech industry with boldness and determination.

As we look to the future of tech, it is clear that these visionaries will continue to shape the industry in bold and daring ways. Their innovative ideas and fearless approach to problem-solving have set them apart as true leaders in Silicon Valley and beyond. For those who aspire to make their mark in the tech industry, these bold entrepreneurs serve as a source of inspiration and a reminder that with confidence and courage, anything is possible.

Breaking Barriers: Tech Trailblazers

In the fast-paced world of technology, there are a select few who stand out as true trailblazers. These individuals are not afraid to take risks, break barriers, and push the boundaries of what is possible. They are the confident and courageous Top of the Field, bold entrepreneurs shaping the future of the tech industry.

These trailblazers are not content to simply follow in the footsteps of those who came before them. They are constantly seeking new challenges and pushing themselves to innovate and create. Their confidence and courage are what set them apart from the rest, allowing them to achieve incredible success in an ever-changing industry.

One such trailblazer is John Smith, the founder of a groundbreaking tech startup that is revolutionizing the way we interact with technology. Smith's bold vision and fearless approach to business have allowed him to break through barriers and achieve success where others have failed. His story is a testament to the power of confidence and courage in the tech industry.

Another tech trailblazer is Sarah Johnson, a fearless entrepreneur who has made a name for herself in the male-dominated world of technology. Johnson's commitment to pushing boundaries and challenging the status quo has made her a force to be reckoned with in the tech industry. Her story is an inspiration to all those who aspire to be bold entrepreneurs in the tech world.

These tech trailblazers serve as examples to all those who dream of making their mark in the tech industry. Their stories show us that with confidence and courage, anything is possible. They are the bold visionaries who are shaping the future of tech, and their legacy will inspire generations of entrepreneurs to come.

By Susette ONeal

11 Chapter Fearless Entrepreneurs

Risk Takers of the Tech Industry

The tech industry is known for being a breeding ground for risk takers and pioneers who are unafraid to push the boundaries of innovation. These bold visionaries are the driving force behind the rapid advancements and breakthroughs that shape our future. In this subchapter, we will delve into the lives and careers of some of the most fearless and daring individuals in the tech industry.

One such risk taker is Elon Musk, the founder and CEO of SpaceX and Tesla. Musk is known for his audacious goals and willingness to take on seemingly impossible challenges. From revolutionizing the electric car industry with Tesla to pushing the boundaries of space exploration with SpaceX, Musk's bold vision and unwavering determination have solidified his status as one of the top entrepreneurs in the tech industry.

Another fearless leader in the tech industry is Jeff Bezos, the founder of Amazon. Bezos took a huge risk by starting an online bookstore in the early days of the internet, but his bold decision paid off in a big way. Today, Amazon is one of the largest and most successful tech companies in the world, thanks to Bezos's fearless approach to innovation and his willingness to take calculated risks.

In addition to Musk and Bezos, there are countless other confident and courageous individuals at the top of the tech industry who are constantly pushing the boundaries of what is possible. These bold entrepreneurs are not afraid to fail and are always willing to take risks in order to achieve their vision of the future.

As males in the tech industry, it is important to take inspiration from these risk takers and embrace the spirit of boldness and innovation that drives them. By following in the footsteps of these fearless leaders, we can continue to push the boundaries of what is possible and shape the future of technology in bold and exciting ways.

Disruptors and Innovators

In the world of technology, disruptors and innovators

play a crucial role in shaping the future. These are the individuals who are not afraid to challenge the status quo and push the boundaries of what is possible. They are the ones who have the vision and determination to create groundbreaking solutions that change the way we live and work. In the book "The Bold Visionaries: Men Shaping the Future of Tech," we highlight some of the most confident and courageous individuals who are at the top of their field, as well as bold entrepreneurs who are taking risks in the tech industry.

One such disruptor is Elon Musk, the founder of SpaceX and Tesla. Musk is known for his ambitious vision of colonizing Mars and revolutionizing the automotive industry with electric cars. Despite facing numerous challenges and setbacks, Musk has persevered and continued to push the boundaries of innovation. His boldness and willingness to take risks have made him a true visionary in the tech industry.

Another innovator featured in the book is Jeff Bezos, the founder of Amazon. Bezos transformed the way we shop online and built one of the largest e-commerce companies in the world. He is known for his relentless focus on customer satisfaction and his willingness to invest in long-term growth, even at the expense of short-term profits. Bezos's bold approach to business has made Amazon a household name and a dominant force in the tech industry.

In addition to these well-known disruptors, the book also highlights lesser-known entrepreneurs who are making waves in the tech industry. These individuals may not have the same level of fame as Musk or Bezos, but they are equally bold and innovative in their own right. From cutting-edge startups to groundbreaking research projects, these entrepreneurs are pushing the boundaries of what is possible in the tech industry and shaping the future in exciting new ways.

"The Bold Visionaries: Men Shaping the Future of Tech" is a celebration of the confident and courageous individuals who are at the forefront of innovation in the tech industry. Whether they are disrupting established industries or creating new ones from scratch, these bold visionaries are changing the world one breakthrough at a time. This book is a must-read for anyone who is inspired by the power of innovation and the potential of technology to transform our lives for the better.

By Susette ONeal

12 Chapter The Rise of the Titans

Tech Titans: Building Empires

In the world of technology, there are certain individuals who have risen to the top, building empires, and shaping the future of the industry. These tech titans are bold visionaries, unafraid to take risks and push the boundaries of what is possible. They are the confident and courageous leaders of the field, inspiring others to follow in their footsteps and innovate in new and exciting ways.

One such tech titan is Elon Musk, the founder of SpaceX and Tesla Motors. Musk is known for his bold vision of colonizing Mars and revolutionizing the automotive industry with electric cars. His fearless approach to business has earned him a reputation as one of the most innovative and daring entrepreneurs of our time.

Another tech titan making waves in the industry is Jeff

Bezos, the founder of Amazon. Bezos has built an empire that has disrupted traditional retail and transformed the way we shop online. His relentless focus on customer satisfaction and willingness to take risks have made Amazon one of the most successful companies in the world.

These tech titans are not afraid to think big and dream even bigger. They are constantly pushing the boundaries of what is possible and inspiring others to do the same. Their bold vision and unwavering confidence have allowed them to build empires that will shape the future of technology for years to come.

For those who aspire to follow in their footsteps, the key is to be bold, take risks, and never be afraid to fail. The tech industry is constantly evolving, and only those who are willing to push the boundaries and challenge the status quo will succeed. So, for the confident and courageous entrepreneurs at the top of the field, the future is bright and full of endless possibilities.

Scaling New Heights: Success Stories

In this subchapter, we will delve into the incredible success stories of bold entrepreneurs who have taken risks in the tech industry and reached new heights of success. These men are the epitome of confidence and courage, pushing boundaries and reshaping the future of technology with their innovative ideas and fearless determination.

One such visionary is Elon Musk, the CEO of SpaceX

and Tesla, Inc. Musk's relentless pursuit of his bold vision to revolutionize space exploration and sustainable energy has earned him a reputation as one of the most daring and ambitious entrepreneurs of our time. From launching rockets into space to developing electric cars that are changing the automotive industry, Musk's fearless approach to innovation has inspired countless others to dream big and aim high.

Another inspiring success story is that of Jeff Bezos, the founder, and CEO of Amazon. Bezos started his journey as a humble online bookstore and transformed it into the e-commerce giant that it is today. His unwavering commitment to customer satisfaction and relentless focus on long-term growth have made Amazon a household name and a driving force in the tech industry. Bezos's bold vision and willingness to take risks have solidified his place as a top leader in the field.

Jack Ma, the co-founder, and former executive chairman of Alibaba Group, is another fearless entrepreneur who has scaled new heights in the tech industry. Ma's bold vision to connect businesses and consumers in China through e-commerce has revolutionized the way people shop and do business. His determination to overcome challenges and push boundaries has made Alibaba one of the largest and most successful tech companies in the world.

These success stories serve as a reminder to all confident and courageous individuals in the tech industry that with bold vision and unwavering determination, anything is possible. By taking risks, pushing boundaries, and embracing innovation, these men have not only shaped the future of technology but have also inspired a new generation of bold entrepreneurs to follow in their footsteps. The sky is the limit for those who dare to dream big and strive for greatness in the ever-evolving world of tech.

13 Chapter The Maverick Minds

Unconventional Thinkers in Tech

In the fast-paced world of technology, it takes more than just technical skills to make a mark. It requires unconventional thinking, the ability to see beyond the status quo and envision a future that others may not even dare to dream of. In this subchapter, we will explore some of the most unconventional thinkers in the tech industry who have defied the odds and pushed the boundaries of what is possible.

One such visionary is Elon Musk, the founder of SpaceX and Tesla. Musk is known for his bold and audacious vision of colonizing Mars and revolutionizing the automotive industry with electric cars. His willingness to take risks and think outside the box has made him a polarizing figure in the tech world, but there is no denying the impact he has had on shaping the future of technology.

Another unconventional thinker in tech is Tim Ferriss, the author of "The 4-Hour Workweek" and host of "The Tim Ferriss Show" podcast. Ferriss is known for his unconventional approach to productivity and success, advocating for strategies that challenge traditional wisdom. His willingness to experiment and take risks has made him a role model for confident and courageous entrepreneurs looking to make a mark in the tech industry.

Peter Thiel is another unconventional thinker in tech who has made a significant impact on the industry. As the co-founder of PayPal and an early investor in Facebook, Thiel has a reputation for thinking outside the box and challenging conventional wisdom. His book "Zero to One" encourages entrepreneurs to think differently and create something truly unique in a world filled with copycats.

These unconventional thinkers in tech serve as an inspiration to confident and courageous individuals who are looking to make their mark in the industry. By challenging the status quo and thinking outside the box, they have reshaped the future of technology and paved the way for a new generation of bold entrepreneurs. As you embark on your own journey in the tech world, remember to embrace your unconventional thinking and never be afraid to take risks. Who knows, you may just be the next bold visionary shaping the future of tech.

Challenging the Status Quo: Bold Moves

In the fast-paced world of technology, challenging the status quo is crucial for success. The most successful and influential men in the tech industry are those who are not afraid to make bold moves and take risks. These visionaries understand that in order to stay ahead of the competition, they must constantly push the boundaries and think outside the box.

For confident and courageous top-of-the-field males in the tech industry, challenging the status quo can lead to groundbreaking innovations and new opportunities for growth. By taking risks and daring to be different, these bold entrepreneurs are able to disrupt the industry and create new trends that others will follow. It is through their fearless approach to business that they are able to carve out their own path and leave a lasting impact on the tech world.

One of the key characteristics of these bold visionaries is their unwavering confidence in their abilities and ideas. They are not afraid to go against the grain and challenge conventional wisdom in order to achieve their goals. This confidence allows them to take calculated risks and make decisions that others may view as too risky or unconventional. By trusting in their own instincts and vision, they are able to forge their own path and create a legacy that will be remembered for years to come.

These men understand that in order to truly make a difference in the tech industry, they must be willing to take risks and challenge the status quo. By doing so, they are able to push the boundaries of what is possible and inspire others to think differently. Their bold moves serve as a reminder to all entrepreneurs that success often comes from taking risks and daring to be different.

For the confident and courageous top-of-the-field males in the tech industry, challenging the status quo is not just a strategy – it is a way of life. By making bold moves and taking risks, these visionaries are able to shape the future of technology and leave a lasting impact on the world. Their fearless approach to business serves as a blueprint for others to follow, inspiring a new generation of entrepreneurs to think outside the box and push the boundaries of what is possible in the tech industry.

By Susette ONeal

14 Chapter The Future of Tech

Trends and Innovations Shaping the Industry

In the rapidly evolving tech industry, trends and innovations are constantly shaping the landscape and pushing boundaries. As confident and courageous top-of-the-field males in the tech industry, it is crucial to stay ahead of these trends in order to remain competitive and successful. This subchapter will explore some of the key trends and innovations that are currently shaping the industry, and how bold entrepreneurs are taking risks to capitalize on these opportunities.

One of the most significant trends in the tech industry is the rise of artificial intelligence (AI) and machine learning. These technologies are revolutionizing the way we work, live, and interact with the world around us. From self-driving cars to personalized recommendations on streaming services, AI is becoming increasingly integrated into our daily lives. As a top-of-the-field male in the tech industry, it is important to understand how AI can be leveraged to improve products and services, and to stay ahead of the curve in this rapidly advancing field.

Another trend that is shaping the tech industry is the increasing focus on cybersecurity. With the rise of cyber-attacks and data breaches, companies are investing more resources into protecting their systems and data. As a bold entrepreneur, it is essential to prioritize cybersecurity in order to safeguard your business and your customers. By staying informed on the latest cybersecurity trends and innovations, you can ensure that your company remains secure and resilient in the face of potential threats.

In addition to AI and cybersecurity, the tech industry is also seeing innovations in areas such as virtual reality, blockchain, and the Internet of Things (IoT). These technologies have the potential to revolutionize industries ranging from healthcare to finance and are creating new opportunities for bold entrepreneurs to disrupt the status quo. By staying informed on these trends and experimenting with new technologies, top-of-the-field males can position themselves as leaders in their respective fields and drive innovation in the tech industry.

In conclusion, the tech industry is constantly evolving, and staying ahead of trends and innovations is essential for confident and courageous males who are striving to be top-of-the-field in their field. By embracing technologies such as AI, cybersecurity, virtual reality, blockchain, and IoT, bold entrepreneurs can position themselves as leaders in the industry and drive innovation that shapes the future of tech. By taking risks and staying informed on the latest trends, these visionary men can make a lasting impact on the tech industry and pave the way for a bold and innovative future.

The Next Generation of Visionaries

In the fast-paced world of technology, the next generation of visionaries is already making their mark. These young men are not afraid to take risks and push the boundaries of innovation. They embody the qualities of confidence and courage that set them apart from the rest.

These bold entrepreneurs are not content with the status quo. They are constantly seeking new ways to disrupt the tech industry and create something truly revolutionary. Their fearless attitude and willingness to take risks have propelled them to the top of their field, where they are making a name for themselves as leaders in their respective industries.

The next generation of visionaries understands the importance of staying ahead of the curve and embracing change. They are always looking for new opportunities to innovate and improve upon existing technologies. Their forward-thinking mindset and willingness to adapt to new challenges make them unstoppable forces in the tech industry.

These young men are not afraid to dream big and set ambitious goals for themselves. They understand that success does not come easy and are willing to put in the hard work and dedication required to achieve their vision. Their relentless drive and determination are what sets them apart from the competition and allows them to thrive in a constantly evolving industry.

As we look to the future of technology, it is clear that these bold visionaries will continue to shape the landscape of the tech industry for years to come. Their innovative ideas and fearless approach to business are what make them the true leaders of tomorrow. The next generation of visionaries is here, and they are ready to change the world.

By Susette ONeal

15 Chapter Lessons from the Masters

Strategies for Success in Tech

In the fast-paced and ever-evolving world of technology, success is not guaranteed. It takes a combination of hard work, determination, and strategic thinking to rise to the top of the field. For males who are confident and courageous top of the field or bold entrepreneurs taking risks in the tech industry, there are several key strategies that can help pave the way to success.

One of the most important strategies for success in tech is to stay curious and continuously learn. The tech industry is constantly changing, with new developments and innovations happening all the time. By staying curious and open to new ideas, you can stay ahead of the curve and position yourself as a leader in the field.

Whether it's attending conferences, taking courses, or

simply reading up on the latest trends, investing in your own education is crucial for success.

Another key strategy for success in tech is to build a strong network of peers and mentors. Surrounding yourself with like-minded individuals who share your passion for technology can provide valuable support and guidance as you navigate the challenges of the industry. Mentors can offer advice, share their experiences, and help you make important connections that can open doors to new opportunities. Building a strong network can also help you stay motivated and inspired, especially during tough times.

In addition to building a strong network, it's important to take calculated risks in order to succeed in the tech industry. Bold entrepreneurs who are willing to take risks are often the ones who achieve the greatest success. Whether it's launching a new product, entering a new market, or pursuing a new business venture, taking risks can lead to big rewards. Of course, it's important to weigh the potential benefits and drawbacks of each risk carefully but being willing to step outside your comfort zone is essential for growth and success.

Another key strategy for success in tech is to build a strong network of peers and mentors. Surrounding yourself with like-minded individuals who share your passion for technology can provide valuable support and guidance as you navigate the challenges of the industry. Mentors can offer advice, share their experiences, and help you make important connections that can open doors to new opportunities. Building a strong network can also help you stay motivated and inspired, especially during tough times.

In addition to building a strong network, it's important to take calculated risks in order to succeed in the tech industry. Bold entrepreneurs who are willing to take risks are often the ones who achieve the greatest success. Whether it's launching a new product, entering a new market, or pursuing a new business venture, taking risks can lead to big rewards. Of course, it's important to weigh the potential benefits and drawbacks of each risk carefully but being willing to step outside your comfort zone is essential for growth and success.

Another important strategy for success in tech is to focus on building strong relationships with clients, colleagues, and industry leaders. In a field as competitive as tech, strong relationships can make all the difference. By providing excellent customer service, collaborating effectively with colleagues, and networking with industry leaders, you can build a reputation as a trustworthy and reliable professional. This can lead to new opportunities, partnerships, and collaborations that can help propel your career to new heights.

It's important to stay adaptable and flexible in the tech industry. The only constant in technology is change, and the ability to adapt to new developments and trends is crucial for success. Whether it's learning a new programming language, mastering a new tool, or pivoting your business strategy in response to market changes, being adaptable can help you stay ahead of the competition and thrive in a dynamic industry. By embracing change and staying flexible, you can position yourself as a bold visionary shaping the future of tech.

Overcoming Challenges and Adversities

In the fast-paced world of technology, challenges and adversities are inevitable. However, it is how we respond to these obstacles that truly defines our success. For males in the tech industry, being confident and courageous is essential in overcoming these hurdles and reaching new heights in their careers. In this subchapter, we will explore the stories of bold entrepreneurs who have faced and conquered challenges, inspiring others to do the same.

One common challenge that many top-of-the-field tech professionals face is the fear of failure. The tech industry is constantly evolving, and taking risks is a necessary part of staying ahead. However, this can be daunting for even the most confident individuals. By embracing failure as a learning opportunity, these bold entrepreneurs have been able to push past their fears and achieve great success.

Another challenge that many males in the tech industry face is imposter syndrome. This feeling of inadequacy can be particularly prevalent in male-dominated fields, where the pressure to constantly perform at a high level can be overwhelming. By recognizing their own worth and capabilities, these entrepreneurs have been able to rise above imposter syndrome and prove their value in the industry.

In addition to internal challenges, external factors can also present obstacles for bold entrepreneurs in the tech industry. From fierce competition to rapidly changing trends, staying relevant can be a constant struggle. However, by remaining adaptable and resilient, these individuals have been able to navigate these challenges and come out on top.

16 Chapter Inspiring Stories of Triumph

From Humble Beginnings to Tech Giants

In the world of technology, many of the most successful companies and entrepreneurs have risen from humble beginnings to become tech giants. These individuals have shown incredible tenacity and determination in pursuing their dreams, and their stories serve as inspiration to all who aspire to reach the top of the tech industry.

One such individual is Jeff Bezos, the founder of Amazon. Bezos started the company in his garage with just a handful of employees, but his bold vision and relentless drive propelled Amazon to become one of the largest and most influential tech companies in the world.

His story is a testament to the power of perseverance and innovation in the face of adversity.

Another example is Mark Zuckerberg, the founder of Facebook. Zuckerberg started the social media platform in his college dorm room, and through his bold and audacious leadership, he transformed Facebook into a global powerhouse that has revolutionized the way we connect and communicate with one another. His story is a reminder that with courage and determination, anything is possible in the tech industry.

Elon Musk is another tech giant who has risen from humble beginnings to become a visionary leader in the industry. Musk founded SpaceX with the goal of making space travel more accessible and affordable, and through his bold and daring approach, he has pushed the boundaries of what is possible in space exploration. His story is a testament to the power of thinking big and taking risks in pursuit of a bold vision.

These individuals, along with many others in the tech industry, have shown that with confidence, courage, and a willingness to take risks, anyone can achieve greatness. Their stories serve as a reminder to all aspiring entrepreneurs that success is possible, no matter where you start from. By following in their footsteps and embracing boldness and innovation, the sky is truly the limit in the world of tech.

Transforming the World with Technology

In today's rapidly evolving world, technology plays a

pivotal role in transforming the way we live, work, and interact with each other. From artificial intelligence to blockchain, the possibilities are endless when it comes to leveraging technology for the greater good. As confident and courageous top-of-the-field males in the tech industry, it is up to us to harness the power of innovation to shape a better future for all.

One of the key ways in which technology is transforming the world is through automation. By automating repetitive tasks and processes, businesses can increase efficiency, reduce costs, and free up employees to focus on more strategic and creative work.

This not only benefits the bottom line but also enables companies to deliver better products and services to their customers, ultimately driving growth and success in the marketplace.

Another area where technology is making a significant impact is in the realm of healthcare. From telemedicine to wearable devices that monitor vital signs, the healthcare industry is embracing technology to improve patient outcomes and reduce costs. As bold entrepreneurs taking risks in the tech industry, we have the opportunity to revolutionize healthcare delivery and make a positive impact on the lives of millions of people around the world.

In addition to automation and healthcare, technology is also transforming the way we communicate and collaborate. With the rise of remote work and virtual meetings, we are no longer bound by physical location when it comes to doing business. This has opened up new opportunities for collaboration and innovation, allowing us to work with talented individuals from around the globe to bring our bold visions to life.

As we continue to push the boundaries of what is possible with technology, it is important to remember the impact that our work can have on society as a whole. By leveraging technology for the greater good, we have the power to create a more connected, efficient, and sustainable world for future generations. Let us embrace the challenge and be the bold visionaries who shape the future of tech for the betterment of all.

17 Chapter The Legacy of Bold Visionaries

Impact on Society and Culture

In the tech industry, the impact on society and culture by bold visionaries cannot be understated. These confident and courageous top-of-the-field individuals are shaping the future in ways that will have lasting effects on our world. From disrupting traditional industries to creating new ways of communication, the influence of these bold entrepreneurs is felt far and wide.

One of the key ways in which these top-of-the-field individuals are impacting society and culture is through their innovative products and services. Whether it's a new app that revolutionizes how we interact with technology or a groundbreaking piece of hardware that changes the way we work, these bold visionaries are constantly pushing the boundaries of what is possible. This innovation not only benefits consumers but also has a ripple effect on other industries, creating new opportunities for growth and development.

Furthermore, the societal impact of these bold entrepreneurs extends beyond just their products. By creating successful tech companies, they are also creating jobs and driving economic growth in their communities. This not only boosts local economies but also helps to inspire the next generation of entrepreneurs to follow in their footsteps. In this way, these individuals are not only changing the tech industry but also shaping the future of business as a whole.

From a cultural standpoint, these bold visionaries are also making waves. By challenging traditional norms and pushing the boundaries of what is possible, they are helping to redefine what it means to be successful in today's world. Their willingness to take risks and think outside the box is inspiring others to do the same, leading to a more diverse and inclusive tech industry.

The impact of these bold visionaries on society and culture cannot be overstated. From their innovative products to their economic contributions, these individuals are shaping the future in ways that will have lasting effects for years to come. As confident and courageous top-of-the-field entrepreneurs, they are leading the charge towards a more innovative and inclusive tech industry, setting the stage for a brighter future for all.

Shaping the Future of Technology

In the fast-paced world of technology, it takes confident and courageous individuals to shape the future of the industry. These bold visionaries are not afraid to take risks, push boundaries, and challenge the status quo. They are the ones who are leading the way in innovation, paving the path for the future of technology.

For males who aspire to be at the top of their field in the tech industry, it is important to embrace the mindset of a bold visionary. This means being willing to take risks, think outside the box, and constantly push yourself to new heights. It also means having the confidence to stand behind your ideas, even when others may doubt you.

One of the key traits of successful tech entrepreneurs is their ability to adapt to change and embrace new technologies. The tech industry is constantly evolving, and those who are not willing to adapt will quickly find themselves left behind. By staying ahead of the curve and being open to new ideas, you can position yourself as a leader in the industry.

In conclusion, the future of technology is collaboration. By sharing knowledge, resources, and ideas, you can create a synergy that propels the industry forward and drives innovation.

18 Chapter Conclusion

As we conclude this transformative journey, I challenge each of you to fully embrace your power as an Alpha Female. Lead with confidence in every aspect of your life, knowing that you are capable of achieving greatness.

Throughout this book, we've delved into the defining traits of an Alpha Female leader and the significance of embodying these qualities to attain success. It is essential to maintain an unwavering belief in yourself and your abilities, even when faced with adversity.

Take a moment to reflect on your leadership journey. Acknowledge the progress you have made and the obstacles you have conquered. Celebrate your triumphs and learn from your setbacks, as both are vital for your growth and development. By recognizing your strengths and areas for improvement, you can continue to hone your leadership skills and become an even more impactful leader.

Set clear goals for your continued growth and success. Inspire those around you to embrace their Alpha Female identity and lead with confidence. Together, we can cultivate a world where Alpha Female leaders thrive and create lasting, meaningful change.

Remember, a woman can possess the grace of a gentle lamb while embodying the inner strength of an unyielding rock. Be both. Embrace your Alpha Female power and make your mark on the world.

In the dynamic world of technology, it takes confident and courageous individuals to shape the industry's future. These bold visionaries are the trailblazers, unafraid to take risks, push boundaries, and challenge the status quo. They lead innovation and pave the path for the future of technology.

For men aspiring to excel in the tech industry, adopting the mindset of a bold visionary is crucial. This involves embracing risk, thinking creatively, and continuously striving for excellence. It means having the confidence to champion your ideas, even in the face of skepticism.

Successful tech entrepreneurs excel because they adapt to change and embrace new technologies. The tech industry evolves rapidly, and those unwilling to adapt risk being left behind. By staying ahead of the curve and welcoming new ideas, you can position yourself as a leader in the industry.

Collaboration is another vital element in shaping the future of technology. No one person holds all the answers, but by working with other visionaries, you can achieve remarkable feats. Sharing knowledge, resources, and ideas creates a synergy that propels the industry forward and drives innovation.

In conclusion, the future depends on confident and courageous individuals willing to take risks, think boldly, and collaborate. By embodying these qualities and relentlessly pursuing new heights, you can establish yourself as a bold visionary in any industry. The opportunities are limitless for those ready to seize them and shape the future.

19 ABOUT THE AUTHOR

Hello there! I'm Susette ONeal, and I hail from the bustling town of Woodbury, NJ. Growing up in a household of 15 children might sound like a chaotic adventure, and let me assure you, it truly was. But in the midst of the chaos, I learned the true meaning of family, love, and the importance of supporting one another. My journey took an unexpected turn when I decided to serve in the military. The discipline, camaraderie, and sense of duty instilled during my service became an integral part of who I am today. I had the privilege of serving alongside some incredible individuals, each with their own unique stories and struggles. One of the most impactful experiences during my military service was gaining a profound understanding of the challenges faced by all Americans. Witnessing the resilience and strength of those who, for various reasons, found themselves in dire crisis' touched my heart. It ignited a passion within me to make a difference and be a voice for those who often go unheard. Today, I channel my experiences and empathy into various community initiatives in North Carolina. In my free time, you'll find me enjoying the simple pleasures of life – spending time with my own family, writing, reading, and exploring the beautiful outdoors.

www.ingramcontent.com/pod-product-compliance
Lightning Source LLC
Chambersburg PA
CBHW070110230526
45472CB00004B/1205